The Earliest Mythicist References

An Edited Compilation and Commentary of Jesus Skeptic References from before Volney and Dupuis.

Second Edition

by

Christopher M. Hansen and Various Others

HANSEN
1872

ASIN: B08DTLB2L3
ISBN: 9798672828671

Published with Kindle Direct Publishing

Second Edition

Christopher M. Hansen is a student and researcher on the history of the so-called "Christ Myth Theory" (CMT) throughout history. Their current main project is the first English language history of the CMT, documenting its progress from past to present, as well as common trends and arguments. Outside of these interests, they study English and are finishing their B.A., and are also socially active for progressive causes, such as Feminism, LGBTQ+ rights, and Racial equality.

TABLE OF CONTENTS

INTRODUCTION

The Christ Myth Theory (CMT) is one of the most historically enigmatic developments in historiographical studies, not least because it is one of the least that is actively studied and analyzed. There are a few reasons for this.

(1) Firstly, it is something that is stigmatized in the consensus of New Testament scholarship. Mark Allan Powell compared them to skinheads, while Walter Weaver is known to have described it as a "lurking monster."[1] In this light, we can see that it is not exactly a prestigious area to actually study, though it is becoming more accepted for this as of late. Academics such as Justin Meggitt (a historicist) have certainly become more open to this debate existing and characterize it as a good thing.[2]

(2) A second aspect of this is that the adherents of the CMT (what I call Jesus Skeptics[3]) have been extremely opposed to any kind of proper historiographical and sociological analysis of their positions. It has become a regular occurrence within their ranks to ultimately dismiss anyone

---

[1] Mark Allan Powell, *Jesus as a Figure in History* (Louisville: Westminster John Knox Press, 1998), 168; Walter P. Weaver, *The Historical Jesus in the Twentieth Century* (Harrisburg: Trinity Press International, 1999), 71.

[2] Justin Meggitt, "Was the Historical Jesus an Anarchist?" in A. Christoyannopoulos and M. S. Adams, *Essays in Anarchism and Religion: Volume 1* (Stockholm: Stockholm University Press, 2017), 125-126 and "'More Ingenious than Learned'? Examining the Quest for the Non-Historical Jesus," *New Testament Studies* 65 (2019): 443-460.

[3] This is an umbrella of atypical scholars and lay historians who argue for non-consensus views on the historicity of Jesus. These include mythicists (reject his historicity altogether), Jesus agnostics (who levy no truth value to the proposition of his existence), temporal historicists (who claim he lived in another time), identity historicists (who claim he was a different person), composite theorists (who think he was a compilation of multiple mythical and/or historical figures), etc. Mythicists and Jesus agnostics have also been called "New Testament Minimalists" by Robert M. Price.

who points out any possible antichristian biases, or other objectively *pertinent* facts about them, often through red herrings or the all too infamous *tu quoqui* fallacy. For instance, in his latest monograph, when confronting this issue, instead of acknowledging these biases or that, yes, many Jesus Skeptics simply are not actually qualified in any way, Lataster instead tries to just pin this on *every single New Testament scholar* and argue that none of them can talk about this issue.[4] There is, most certainly, an aura of overt defensiveness. Oddly enough, this is despite mythicists such as Y. A. Lenzman and Iosif A. Kryvelev even making a point to discuss that, yes, Jesus Skeptics were (and are) biased in favor of their positions.[5]

Because of this being such a hot button issue, historiographical work on the CMT has been, unfortunately, lacking. By far the most complete attempt up to the current date was by Arthur Drews (1865-1935), who traced it from Volney up to his present time, in France, England, the Netherlands, and Germany.[6] Other historiographical work has been severely limited in size and scope, usually just a few pages in an introduction to a wider work, or a single chapter.[7]

---

[4] Raphael Lataster, *Questioning the Historicity of Jesus: Why a Philosophical Analysis Elucidates the Historical Discourse* (Leiden: Brill | Rodopi, 2019), 3-12.

[5] Y. A. Lenzman, "Izucheniye sovetskimi uchenymi rannego khristianstva," *Voprosy nauchnogo ateizma* 4 (1967): 284; Iosif A. Kryvelev, *Christ: Myth or Reality?* "Religious Studies in the USSR" Series (Moscow: USSR Academy of Sciences and "Social Sciences Today" Editorial Board, 1987), 75-80.

[6] Arthur Drews, *Die Leugnung der Geschichtlichkeit Jesu in Vergangenheit und Gegenwart* (Karlsruhe, 1926).

[7] Bart Ehrman, *Did Jesus Exist? The Historical Argument for Jesus of Nazareth* (New York: HarperOne, 2012), 14-19. By far the most detailed by those who have rebutted to the CMT adherents is found in Robert van Voorst, *Jesus Outside the New Testament: An Introduction to the Ancient Evidence* (Grand Rapids: Eerdmans, 2000), 6-16. One should take caution regardless, however, since it still makes a number of errors (such as linking

Often times, it only comes in at just brief asides or short mentions as well.[8] As such, we are in a situation which calls for a decidedly more critical approach to historiography.

Of the works we do have on this, we should also take heed of the critique by Meggitt, that these works have often only looked for explicit mentions, which has left a lot of material completely unheard of and unnoticed.[9] Thus, even with the documentation we have, it is exceedingly weak and incomplete. It is the view of the present author that this demands remedy and correction, especially if scholarship is to ever critically engage with the issue.

The present volume is a companion to a greater work of which I have already finished the first draft. The texts in question come from a variety of backgrounds and languages, but primarily English, French, and German. These all date from the late 1500's (for Trypho, see the Appendix) on up to the time of Volney's writing of *Les Ruines* in 1792, which means that these are all particularly early, especially for discussion of the historicity of Jesus in the negative. As such, some of these may come as somewhat surprising. It must be

---

mythicism to W. C. van Manen, A. D. Loman [who switched back to historicity], and Karl Marx). For a better review of the Dutch Radicals, see Hermann Detering, *Inszenierte Fälschungen: Die Paulusbriefe in der holländischen Radikalkritik* (Independently Published, 2017), 22-118 and for more accurate review of the USSR and Czech debates on Jesus, see Dalibor Papoušek, "The Soviet School of Historians of Early Christianity and Its Influence in Former Czechoslovakia: The Question of Jesus' Historicity," in Iva Doležalová, Luther H. Martin and Dalibor Papoušek (eds.), *The Academic Study of Religion During the Cold War: East and West* (New York: Peter Lang, 2001), 119-135.

[8] Robert Van Voorst, "Nonexistence Hypothesis," in Leslie Houlden (ed), *Jesus in History, Thought, and Culture: An Encyclopedia* (Santa Barbara: ABC-Clio, 2003), 658-660; Michael McClymond, *Familiar Stranger: An Introduction to Jesus of Nazareth* (Grand Rapids: Eerdmans, 2004), 23-24; Jan A. B. Jongeneel, *Jesus Christ in World History* (Frankfurt am Main: Peter Lang, 2009), 172, 209-210, 219, 255-256, 307.

[9] Meggitt, "'More Ingenious than Learned'?", 450-455.

stated that most of these are appearing to come directly from the Jesus Skeptics themselves, however. We do not have their texts (save a few) as far as I am currently aware, and instead are reading responses that came about. Despite this, we can still get an image of what was going on in the world by the fact that they were receiving this attention. In addition to actual responses, we also a series of polemics and items which may or may not be polemics but are practically impossible to tell. As such, it is necessary that I must provide commentary on these texts, thus, the reader will have to indulge me. Translations are mine throughout this work unless noted otherwise.

Thus, it is without further ado that I now end this introduction and allow my readers on to what they came for, the earliest references to those who doubted the historicity of Jesus.

I must thank, beforehand, Justin Meggitt for the publication of his 2019 paper which exposed to the world several works which were otherwise lost to us.[10]

---

[10] Meggitt, "'More Ingenious than Learned'?", 450-455.

Henry More (1614-1687) was an English theologian and a Platonist of the Cambridge variety, who was particularly taken with concepts of mechanical philosophy (Descartes), though he rejected Descartes' dualism. Intriguingly, he would later have an influence on the works of theosophists, including H. Blavatsky in centuries after. However, he is most remembered here for attesting to the early presence of skeptics over Jesus' existence.

Relevant Passages

5. For the firmer belief whereof, he may also help himself something from those strinklings[1] that are found in profane Writers. For if thou wilt be so prodigiously melancholick **[=melancholic]** and suspicious as to doubt whether there ever were such a man as Christ, the very History of the Heathens may assure thee thereof; they mentioning these things so timely, as that there could be no errour about the existence of the Person they speak of whether he ever were in the World or no. For *Plinie* **[=Pliny the Younger]**, *Tacitus*, *Lucian* and *Suetonius*, all of them flourished so near the time of the taking of the City of *Jerusalem* (viz, *Plinie* about twenty, *Tacitus* about thirty, *Lucian* and *Suetonius* about forty or fifty years) that they could not but have certain information whether he was a fictitious Person or real, from the captive *Jews*, who

---

[1] A "sprinkling" roughly, as in "a sprinkling of X."

would not have failed to stifle a Religion they hated so, if it had been but a Figment at the bottome [=**bottom**], *Plinie* in his Epistle to *Trajan*[2] finds the Christian professours in good ernest, even to death; Whose dangerous and mischievous errour he might easily have confuted, if the History of Christ had been but a *Romance*; but he found them immovable, nor could he help it. Which constancy of theirs he calls *pervicacium & inflexibilem obstinationem, a Pervicacity and inflexible obstinacy.* Which is ridiculous to think can befall men in a mere Fiction within the time that search may easily discover to be false, and that they should stand out to the exposing of themselves to death and torture. He writes in the same Epistle that he put two maid-servants on the rack, *Sed nihil aliud inveni quam superstitionem pravam & immodicam, But I found nothing else* (saith he) *but a perverse and immoderate superstition.* And of those that fear made desist from the profession of their Religion, *Affirmabant bant fuisse summam vel culpe sue vel erroris, quod essent soliti slato die ante lucem convenire, carmenque Christo quasi Deo dicere, &c. They affirmed that this was the sum of their either fault or errour, that they were wont on a set day to meet together early in the morning before daybreak, and sing an hymne* [=**hymn**] *to Christ as to a God.* Which is a sign that betimes the Christians followed Christ, not as a mere eminent Moaralist, that gave excellent precepts of life, better than ever any did, but that they held his Person truely [=**truly**]

---

[2] Pliny the Younger, *Epistulae* X.96.

Divine, and adorable for some wonderful considerations or other.

6. But this Inquisition and bloudy [=**bloody**] Persecution of the Christians began higher than *Trajan's* time, to wit in *Nero's*, who, to smother that abominable of his in firing the City of *Rome*, did most savagely punish the Christians, as if they had been the Authors of it. *Tacit.* Annal.lib.15. *Ergo abolendo rumori* Nero *subdidit reos, & quesitissimis poenis affecit, quos per flagitia invisos vulgus* Christianos *appellabat. Auctor nominis ejus* [=**eius**] Christus, *qui* Tiberio *imperitante, per Procuratorem* Pontium Pilatum *supplicio affectus erat. Repressaque in praesens exitabilis superstitio rursus erumpebat, non modo per* Judaeam *originem ejus* [=**eius**] *mali, sed per urbem etiam, quo cuncta undiq; atrocia aut pudenda confluunt celebranturque. Igitur primo correpti qui fatebantur; deinde indicio corummultitudoingens, haud perinde in crimine incendii quam odio humani generis, convicti sunt. Et pereuntibus addita ludibria, ut ferarum tergis contecti laniatu canum interirent, aut flammandi; atque, ubi defecisset dies, in usum nocturni luminis urerentur.* Wherefore, Nero, *to suppress the rumour of his own vile act, by suborning false witnesses got those to be accused who being hateful for their wickedness were commonly called* Christians, *and punished them with exquisite tortures. The Author of that sect was one* Christus, *who in the reign of* Tiberius *was put to death by* Pontius Pilate *the Deputy. Which damnable superstition for a time, broke out afresh, not only in* Judea *the*

first source of that Mischief, but also in the City of Rome, whither all villainous and shameful things flow from all parts, and are held in great esteem. Wherefore they were first laid hold of that confessed *themselves* Christians; *afterward by their discovery a huge multitude were condemned, not so much for being guilty of firing the City, as that they were hated of all mankind. They added also reproaches to their death, clothing some of them with the skins of beasts, to be worried by dogs; others were crucified, and others were burnt after day-light, to serve in stead of lynks[3] or torches.* This persecution was not thirty years after the Passion of Christ. I appeal now to any one, if he can think it possible that these lived so near to that time when Christ was said to be crucified, that they might make *exact* inquiry into the matter; I appeal to him, if he can think it possible they could expose their lives and fortunes to the hatred and cruelty of the Heathen, if they were not most certain that there was such a man that was crucified at *Jerusalem*: and demand further, he dying so ignominious a death, whether it be again possible that there should not be some extraordinary thing in the Person of Christ, to make them adhere to him so after his death, with the common hatred of all men and hazard of their lives.

[continues with discussion of Lucian (paragraph 7), Suetonius (paragraph 8) and Josephus (paragraph 9), and then discussing

---

[3] Lynks are apparently some type of fire for light in this context.

Chapter 10

1. These Testimonies out of Heathen Writers may suffice to take off that fond and groundless suspicion of the whole History of Christ being a mere Allegory or Fiction. A thing that the greatest Enemies thereof had never the face to object to the Christians, neither *Jews* nor *Pagans*, nor our modern Atheists, especially the more nasute[4] sort of them, such as *Pomponatius* and *Vaninus*, who do not only acknowledge Christ's person, but his Miracles; only forsooth they referre [=**refer**] them to the influence of the Stars and celestial Intelligences, of which I shall speak in its proper place. The *Jews* acknowledge his *Miracles* but add that he was a *Magician*: And *Julian* himself and *Celsus*, who wrote against the Christians, never once had the face to deny but that *Jesus* of Nazareth did once live in *Judea*, and did strange things; though the one revolted from him, and the other never believed in him.[5]

Commentary. Here we have reference early on, 1660, to people who rejected or were doubting the historicity of Jesus.

---

[4] An antiquated term designating someone who may be described as "sharp" or "witty".

[5] Henry More, *An Explanation of the Grand Mystery of Godliness: Or, A True and Faithfull Representation of the Everlasting Gospel of Our Lord and Saviour Jesus Christ, the Onely Begotten Son of God and Sovereign Over Men and Angels* (London: J. Flesher, 1660), 315-320.

In this case, More states clearly that this was already a more commonly developing trend within skeptical camps, and as such we may be wondering what literature exists out there, possibly, which may attest to these various skeptics.

There are, in addition, a number of noteworthy elements to his argumentation. Here, More makes heavy use of extrabiblical sources (as most scholars of the time did when addressing this issue), arguing that based on their testimony the historicity of Christ would be firmly established. His discussion is relatively thorough of these sources, though not commenting on the Talmudic ones (see Owen's response to skeptics which does, below). In addition, there are a few textual variants worth noting, including *Christus qui Tiberio*, and *rursus* (cf. in Evans).[6]

---

[6] Cf. Craig Evans, "Jesus in Non-Christian Sources," in Bruce Chilton and Craig A. Evans (eds.), *Studying the Historical Jesus: Evaluations of the State of Current Research* (Leiden: Brill, 1994), 464.

John Owen (1616-1683) was English theologian and what is called a "Nonconformist" who taught at the University of Oxford. He wrote chiefly on various historical events, such as the Restoration of the Stuart monarchy and also ended up in a debate with Edward Stillingfleet (next chapter) on the issues of the Nonconformist faith versus Stillingfleets more stringent protestant one. The following excerpt is from his work entitled, *Exercitations on the Epistle to the Hebrews, Also Concerning the Messiah* (published in 1668).

Relevant Passages[1]

We ask them then, *If Jesus of Nazareth* be not the *Messiah*, where is he? or who is he that came in answer to the Prophecies insisted upon? Two things then remain to be proved. First, That our *Lord Jesus Christ* came, lived, and dyed **[=died]** within the time limited for the coming of the *Messiah*. Secondly, That no other came within that season, that either pretended without any colour of probability unto that dignity, or was ever such, owned or esteemed by the *Jews* themselves.

First then, that Jesus came and lived in the time limited unto the coming of the *Messiah*, some short space of time before the departure of *Scepter* and *Scribe* from *Judah*, the ceasing of the daily Sacrifice, and final desolation of the Second Temple, we have all

---

[1] Aside from updated spelling I shall occasionally be interjecting in brackets [] more current spellings for words and in footnotes providing commentary on lesser known ones.

the evidence, that a matter of fact so long passed, is capable of as good, as that the world was of old by God created. The Stories of the *Church* are express, that he was born during the reign of *Augustus Caesar*, in the latter end of the reign of *Herod* over *Judea*, when *Cyrenius* was governor over *Syria*; that he lived unto the time, wherein *Pontius Pilate* was Governour of *Judea* under *Tiberius*, about thirty six or thirty seven before the destruction of the Nation, City and Temple by *Titus*. This the stories written by *Divine Inspiration*, and committed to the care of the Church, expressly confirm; neither have the Jews any thing to object against the truth of the relation, what ever thoughts they have of this Person, who he was, or what he did: That he lived and dyed **[=died]** then, and there, is left testified on Records beyond controll **[=control]**. And if they should deny it, what is the *bare negation* of a few interested, blinded persons, without Testimonies or evidence from any one circumstance of Times, Persons, or Actions to be laid in ballance **[=balance]** against the *Catholick Tradition* **[=Catholic]** of all the world, whether believing in Jesus, or rejecting him. For they all alwayes **[=always]** consented in this, that he lived, and died at the time mentioned in the sacred stories.

And this was still one part of the charge managed against his followers, in the very next *Age* after, that they believed in a person whom they knew to live at such a season, and in a mean condition. Neither did the most malicious and fierce impugners of the Religion taught by him, such as *Celsus, Porphyrie* **[=Porphyry]**, and *Julian* attempt to attacque [=**attack**] the Truth of the story, as to his real existence, and the time of it. So that herein we have as concurrent a suffrage as the whole world in any case is able to afford.

The best of the *Historians* of the Nations, who lived near those times, give their Testimony unto what is recorded in our Gospel. The words of one of them, a person of unquestionable credit, in things that he could attain the knowledge of, and as it will appear by them, far enough from any compliance with the followers of *Jesus*, may suffice for instance. This is *Cornelius Tacitus*, in the fifteenth of his *Annals*: *Abolendo* (Saith he) *rumori* (he speaks of *Nero* and his firing of *Rome*,) *subditit reos, & quaesitissimis poenis affecit, quos per flagitia invisos vulgus Christianos appellebat. Author ejus* [=*eius*] *nominis Christus qui Tiberio imperitante per procuratorem Puntium Pilatum supplicio affecius erat.*[2] He expressly assignes [=**assigns**] the time of the death of Christ unto the reign of *Tiberius*, and government of *Pilate*. The same is also confirmed by the *Jews* own *Historian Flavius Josephus*, in the fourth *Chapter* of the eighteenth *Book* of their *Antiquities*; unto which season also he assigns[3] the death of *John the Baptist*, who was his contemporary, according to the *Evangelical* Story.[4]

---

[2] Tacitus, *Annals* 15.44.

[3] Note the variant spelling of "assigns" in here (lacking the -*es* ending seen previously).

[4] Josephus, *Antiquities of the Jews*. For Jesus see 18.3.3 mentioned here and also John the Baptist on 18.5.2.

Further, We have that Testimony in this matter, which though in its self, it be of little or no moment, yet as unto them with whom we have to do, is cogent above all others; and this is their own confession. They acknowledge in the *Talmud*, that he lived before the desolation of the *Second Temple*, for they tell us, *cap. Cheleck, and* עד*----cap.*2 that he was the Son of *Pandira* and *Stada*, and that he lived in the dayes [=**days**] of the *Maccabees, Alexander, Hireannus*, and *Aristobulus*, under whom he was crucified. I confess Galatinus, Reuchlinus, and of late the learned Schiklard with some others do contend that it is not *Jesus Christ* whom they intend in the wicked Story which they tell of that *Jesus* the Son of *Pandira*. But the reasons they insist on, are of no cogency to procure the assent of any one, acquainted with their Writings; no the latter *Jews* themselves (ashamed of the prodigious lyes [=**lies**] of their fore-fathers, and affraid [=**afraid**] to own their blasphemies, for fear of provoking Christians against them) do saintly (some of them) deny him to be the person intended. The names of their *Parents* say they agree not. The Lord *Jesus* was the reputed Son of *Joseph*, the true Son of *Mary*. This *Jesus* of the *Talmud*, was the Son of *Pandira* and *Stada*. I shall not reply that *Damascenus lib. 4.* placeth a *Panther*, and *Barpanther*, on the *Genealogie* [=**Genealogy**] of Christ, making the latter Grand-father to the blessed Virgin, seeing it is evident that he borrowed that part of his *Genealogie* from some corrupt Traditions of the *Jews*.[5]

---

[5] John Owen, Exercitations on the Epistle to the Hebrews, Also Concerning

Commentary. This passage is the earliest which I have found which defends the historicity of Jesus through usage of the Talmud. The passage itself is in debate to the "bare negation of a few" whom he declares have no evidence to support their side. Owen, in this passage, also makes standard usage of *Annals* 15.44, which was exceptionally common for scholars wishing to quickly refute the assertions that Christ did not live.

A number of the arguments used here are still standard among apologists today, especially those which attempt to place much weight on the non-Christian testimonies to the historicity of Jesus. It is of particular interest that Owen acknowledges the time discrepancy that the Talmud places on Jesus, since it is in direct contradiction to one of his main arguments, that Jesus lived in a set time for the Messiah's arrival. Of course, one can also note much of the blatant antisemitism present in this text as well.

the Messiah (London: Printed for Various Persons, 1660), 209-210.

Edward Stillingfleet (1635-1699) was a bishop of the Anglican Church who was particularly known for being one of the first major theologians to take on the growing "problem" of deists rising up in the country and questioning the truth of Christianity.[1] In a text dated 1675 but actually published in 1677 entitled *A Letter to a Deist*, Stillingfleet launched a detailed multi-page retort over the historicity of the New Testament narratives of Jesus' life, with explicit statements that have earned it detailed commentary in this work.

Relevant Passages[2]

3. Men that made it their design to deceive the World, if they had thought it necessary to bring in any matter of *Story* concerning the *Author* of their *Religion*, would have placed it at such *a distance of Time*, that it was not capable of being disproved: As it is apparent in the *Heathen Mythology*; for the Stories were such, as no Person could ever pretend to confute them, otherwise than by the inconsistency of them with the common Principles of *Religion*. But if we suppose *Christianity* to have been a meer **[=mere]** device, would the *Apostles* have been so senseless to have laid the main Proof of

---

[1] Richard H. Popkin, "Polytheism, Deism, and Newton," in J. E. Force and R. H. Popkin, *Essays on the Context, Nature, and Influence of Isaac Newton's Theology* (Dordrecht: Kluwer Academic Publishers, 1990), 34; James Malcolm Byrne, *Religion and the Enlightenment: From Descartes to Kant* (Louisville: Westminster John Knox Press, 1998), 108.

[2] Aside from using current lettering, I have maintained the spellings of the original. Where words seem obscure, I shall note in [ ] the meanings for the reader. I have also maintained the original italics and capitalizations.

their *Religion* on a thing which was newly acted, and which they were very capable of enquiring into all the Circumstances that related to it, *viz.* the *Resurrection of Christ from the Dead*? We may see by the whole design of the *New Testament*, the great stress of *Christianity* was laid upon the Truth of this; to this, *Christ* himself appealed before hand: To this all the *Apostles* refer as the might confirmation of their Religion; and this they deliver as a thing which themselves had seen, and had conversed with him for 40 days together, with all the demonstrations imaginable of a *true* and *real Body*: And that not one or two credulous Persons, but so many of them who were hard to be satisfied, and one, not without the most sensible Evidence; but besides these, they tell us of 500 *at once saw him. whereof many were then living*, when those things were Written. Now I pray tell me what *Religion* in the World ever put it self upon so fair a Tryal [=**Trial**] as this? Of a plain Matter of Fact, as capable of being attested as any could be.

Why did not *Amida*, or *Brahma*, or *Xaca*, or any other of the Authors of the present *Religions* of the *East-Indies*? Why did not *Orpheus*, or *Numa*, or any other Introducers of *Religious* Customs among the *Greeks* or *Romans*? Or *Mahomet* [=**Muhammed**] among the *Arabians*, put the issue of the Truth of their *Religion*, on such a plain and easie [=**easy**] *Trial*[3]as this? If you say, *That Christ appeared*

---

[3] It is curious here that Stillingfleet uses the modern spelling of "trial" instead. Previously he used the antiquated *tryal*. An interesting indication

only to his Friends, who were ready to believe such things, and not among his Enemies: I answer, That though they were his *Friends*, yet they were very hard to be perswaded **[=persuaded]** of the *Truth* of it at first; and afterwards gave larger Testimonies of their Fidelity than the Testimony of the greatest *Enemies* would have been; for we should have had only their *bare Words* for it, (if they would have given that, which is very questionable, considering their dealing with the other *Miracles of Christ*:) But the *Apostles* manifested their *Sincerity* by all real Proofs that could be thought sufficient to satisfie **[=satisfy]** Mankind; appealing to the very Persons who were concerned the most in it, having a hand in the Death of *Christ*, declaring their greatest readiness to suffer any thing rather than deny the Truth of it, and laying down their Lives at last for it. If all this had been a meer **[=mere]** Fiction, how unlikely is it, that among so many as were conscious of it, no one Person by Hopes or Fears, by Flatteries or Threatenings, could ever be prevailed upon to deny the Truth of it? If there had been any such thing, what Triumphing had there been among the *Jews*; and no doubt his Name had been Recorded to Posterity, among the Writers, both of *Jews* and *Gentiles*, that were professed Enemies of *Christianity*? But they are all wonderfully silent in this matter; and instead of saying enough to overthrow the *Truth of Christianity*, as you seem to suggest, I do assure you, I am mightily confirmed in the Belief of the Truth of it, by

that the spellings may have been in flux.

carefully observing the slightness of the Objections that were made against it, by its most professed enemies.

But you seem to imply, *That all this Story concerning Christ was invented long after the pretended time of his being in the World*. Why may not you as well suspect, that *Julius Caesar* lived before *Romulus*, or that *Augustus* lived at the Siege of *Troy*? For you might as well reject all History upon such Grounds as those you assign; and think *Mahomet* [=**Muhammed**] as right in his *Chronology*, as the *Bible*. It is time for us to burn all our *Books*, if we have lived in such a Cheat all this while. Methinks you might as well ask, whether *Lucretia* were not *Pope Joan*? Or *Alexander* the *Sixth*, one of the *Roman Emperors*? For there is no greater evidence of any History in the World, than there is, that all the things reported in the *New Testament* were done at the time, when they are pretended to be.[4]

4. Therefore we offer this Story of the *New Testament* to be compared with all the *Circumstances of that Age*, delivered by any other *Historians*, to try if any *Inconsistencies*

---

[4] The term "pretended" here is being used in an antiquated fashion not quite in line with how we perceive it today. Today we assume it means to act out a fiction or play. We "pretend" to be something we are not. However, in an obsolete form it can (and here does) instead carries the meaning of "putting forward for consideration" or "offer" or "presented", see "pretend, v.". OED Online. June 2020. Oxford University Press. https://www-oed-com/view/Entry/150938?rskey=Jvx3pd&result=1 (accessed July 28, 2020). On the converse, it is used in the negative sense at the beginning of the paragraph when Stillingfleet addresses the Deist's implications directly.

can be found therein: Which is the most reasonable way can be taken to disprove any History. If it could be proved, that there could be no *Taxation* of the *Empire* as is mention'd [=**mentioned**] in the time of *Augustus*, that *Herod* did not live in that *Age*, or that the *Jews* were not under the *Roman Government*, or that there were no *High Priests* at that time, nor the *Sects* of *Pharisees* and *Saducees*, or that there were any other remarkable *Characters* of time set down in the *History* of the *New Testament*, which could be manifestly disproved; there were some pretence to call in Question the Truth of the Story; but there is not the least Foundation for any scruple on this account; All things agreeing so well with the truest we have of that *Age*, both from *Josephus* and the *Roman History*. I shall not insist on the particular *Testimony of Josephus* concerning *Christ*, because we need it not;[5] and if those who question it, would proceed with the same severity against many other particular Passages in good *Authors*, they might as well call them in question as they do that; since it is confessed that all Ancient *Manuscripts* have it in them, and supporting that it doth not come in well, must we suppose it impossible for *Josephus* to Write incoherently? Yet this is the main Argument that ever I have seen urged against this *Testimony* of *Josephus*. But I say, we need it not; all other things concurring in so high a degree to prove the *Truth of the History* of *Christ*. Yet since you seem to express so much

---

[5] Here Stillingfleet references Josephus, *Antiquities of the Jews* 18.3.3, better known today as the *Testimonium Flavianum*.

doubtfulness concerning it, *as though it were framed when there was no one living capable of disproving it*; give me leave to shew [=**show**] you the great absurdity of such a Supposition. 1. Because we have the plain Testimonies of the greatest Enemies of *Christianity*, that there was such a Person as *Christ* was, who suffered according to the *Scripture-Story*. For *Tacitus* not only mentions the *Christians* as suffering at *Rome* for their *Religion* in the *time* of *Nero*, (*Annal.* 15) but faith, *That the Author of this Religion was one Christ, who suffered under* Pontius Pilate, *procurator of* Judea, *in the time of* Tiberius;[6] which is an irrefragable Testimony of the *Truth* of the Story concerning *Christ*, in an *Age*, when if it had been false, nothing could have been more easily detected than such a Fiction, by the number of *Jews* which were continually at *Rome*: And neither *Julian*, nor *Celsus*, nor *Porphyrie* [=**Porphyry**], nor *Lucian*, did ever question the *Truth* of the Story it self; but only upbraided[7] the *Christians* for attributing too much to *Christ*. 2. If there were really such a Person as Christ was, who suffered as *Tacitus* saith, then the whole Story could not be a Fiction, but only some part of it; and these additional parts must either be contrived by the *Apostles*, or after their time: Not after their time, for then they must be added after *Christianity* was received in the World, for that, as appears by *Tacitus*,

---

[6] Here Stillingfleet produces a partial quotation of Tacitus, *Annals* 15.44.

[7] This is an antiquated term meaning to "find fault" or "scold" another. Somewhat similar, but not as forceful, as the terms "berate" and "attack" when used in a literary sense.

was spread in the *Apostles* times as far as *Rome*; and if these parts were not received with it; the Cheat would presently have been discover'd [=**discovered**] as soon as broached, by those who had embraced *Christianity* before: And besides, *Tertullian* in his time appeals to the *Authentick*[8] *Writings* of the *Apostles* themselves, which were then extant, wherein the same things were contained that we now believe: If these things then were forged, it must be by the *Apostles* themselves; and I dare now appeal to you, whether ever any Story was better capable of being disproved than this was, if it had not been true, since it was published in the very time and place, where the *Persons* were living, who were most concerned to disprove it: As appears by the hatred of the *Jews* to the *Christians*, both then and ever since: Which is a very observable Circumstance for proving the *truth* of *Christian Religion*; for the *Jews* and *Christians* agreed in the *Divine Revelations* of old, the *Christians* believed moreover, that *Christ* was the *Messias* [=**Messiah**] promised; this *Christ* lived and dyed [=**died**] among the *Jews* his Enemies; his *Apostles* Preached, and wrought Miracles among their most inveterate[9] Enemies, which Men that go about to deceive never care to do: And to this Day the *Jews* do not deny the *Matters* of *Fact*, but look on them as insufficient to prove *Jesus* of *Nazareth* to have

---

[8] Antiquated spelling of "authentic."

[9] Another antiquated term, roughly meaning to have a "habit" or "activity" that will not change, i.e. these "Enemies" are eternally compulsive in their attempt to oppose Christianity.

been the *Messias* [=**Messiah**]: Nay, *Mahomet* himself, who in all probability would have overthrown the whole Story of the *New Testament*, if he could have done it with any colour, yet speaks very honourably of *Christ* and of the great things which were said and done by him.[10]

Commentary. It is unfortunate that we do not know precisely who Stillingfleet was responding to in such detail. Meggitt (who alerted the present author to this text in his 2019 paper) suggests that this could be the Herbert of Cherbury.[11] Unfortunately, we will likely never know to whom this originally referred, unless by some happenstance we were to find the personal notes of Stillingfleet where he laid this out. Of a greater loss is that we do not have the original work or details of the theory of the referent of this piece. As such, we are left with only being able to somewhat guess as to what this deist was implying originally.

There are firstly a number of noteworthy elements here. Firstly, already in the late 17th century, the *Testimonium Flavianum* was already being doubted as authentic, and Stillingfleets brief comments saying that he does not need it may, perhaps, imply the deist adamantly dismissed it. On the converse *Annals* 15.44 by Tacitus was not seen as specious by most authorities yet.[12] As such, Stillingfleet is able to use it as

---

[10] Edward Stillingfleet, *A Letter to a Deist, in Answer to Several Objections against the Truth and Authority of the Scriptures* (London: W. G., 1677), 43-54.

[11] Justin Meggitt, "'More Ingenious Than Learned'? Examining the Quest for the Non-Historical Jesus," *New Testament Studies* 65 (2019): 443-460, particularly 454n77.

[12] Today it is not either except by a handful of (mostly mythicist) figures. For the most recent attempt, see Richard Carrier, "The Prospect of a Christian Interpolation in Tacitus, *Annals* 15:44," *Vigilae Christianae* 68 (2014): 1-20. For its refutations, see Ivan Prchlík, "Auctor Nominis Eius

a rebuttal and claim that there was such a person as Christ who lived in the time ascribed to him. This argument in particular is telling of what this deist apparently argued (at least in implication), as Stillingfleet would have no logical reason to justify the existence of Jesus had there been no such argument which, at least implied, cast aspersions on his historicity.

We should note that this deist, then, would not be writing in a vacuum either. The doubts against the authenticity of various works, including those which attest to Jesus, were not uncommon. Many will now be more familiar with the work of Jean Hardouin (1646-1729), recently re-edited and published by the late Hermann Detering.[13] However, it also appears that the Dutch theologian Conrad Vorstius (1569-1622) was among those who would doubt the authenticity of various works and passages which were ascribed to Christ.[14] While Hardouin was too devout to cast doubts on the historicity of the Biblical narratives (particularly of the Vulgate), this deist seems to have had no such limits, ascribing the whole narrative of the New Testament a level of fiction or fabrication, written long after Jesus supposedly lived.

The rebuttals by Stillingfleet are notable here for being firstly very polemical and secondly also very predictive of many apologetic arguments today. The common rebuttal that Jesus is one of the best attested figures in history, with comparisons to Tiberius, for example, directly foreshadow

---

Christus. Tacitus' knowledge of the origins of Christianity," *Philologica 2/ Graecolatina Pragensia* (2017): 95-110 and Willem Blom, "Why the Testimonium Taciteum Is Authentic: A Response to Carrier," *Vigiliae Christianae* 73, no. 5 (2019): 564-581

[13] Jean Hardouin (au.) and Hermann Detering (ed.), *Prolegomena*, trans. Edwin Johnson (Independently Published, 2017), ori. trans. in 1909 and ori. book published in 1729, the year Hardouin died.

[14] Anonymous author, "Historical and Critical Reflections on Mahometanism and Socinianism," in *Four Treatises concerning the Doctrine, Discipline and Worship of the Mahometans* (London: B. Lintott, 1712), 196-197.

figures such as Sean McDowell and their factually errant positions attempting to say Jesus is better attested than Jesus.[15] However, there is a rather poignant aspect to this, for the time, in that Stillingfleet is discussing (on a meta level) the standards of evidence used to decide what is or is not history, and clearly he has a concept of the *criteria of multiple attestation*, in how he attempts to corroborate the New Testament with pagan accounts about Jesus as well. As such, we can very much look at this as, for the time, a rather innovative argument.

As for the deist, I would hesitantly reconstruct his arguments as roughly following this outline:

1) The New Testament is fabricated history occurring long after the events that it portrays.
2) Non-Christian accounts do not corroborate Jesus' life, through the dismissal of Josephus.
3) Jesus as a historical person is in question.[16]

As such, this would be the first Jesus Skeptic with a described position and rebuttal made in any lengthy treatment.

---

[15] For details, see Christopher M. Hansen, "The Evidence for Jesus, or, Why Sean McDowell is a Wolf in a Historian's Clothing," *Questions for Jesus* (2020), https://cmepshansen9.wixsite.com/mysite/post/the-evidence-for-jesus-or-why-sean-mcdowell-is-a-wolf-in-a-historian-s-clothing.

[16] Whether or not he argued he definitely did not exist (mythicist) or whether we simply do not know if he did or not (Jesus Agnostic) is unknown.

Thomas Woolston (1668-1733) was an English theologian, often categorized as a deist though some debate exists, who is primarily relevant to this debate because of his *Six Discourses on Miracles*, which were published from 1727-1730. In these texts, we have numerous veiled and complex discussions on the historicity of the New Testament and some of the most outlandish exegesis ever accomplished by a modern theologian, which has also caused some stir as to how to take these texts. We shall get to the debate on how he takes the historical Jesus below.

Relevant Statement.

And in truth it was a most astonishing one, if literally true, and Jesus must appear more than a Man, he must put on an awful and most Majestick [=**majestic**] Countenance to effect it. It is hard to conceive, how any one in the Form of a Man, and of a despised one too, (and we don't read that Jesus chang'd [=**changed**] his human shape) with a Whip in his Hand could execute such a Work upon a great Multitude of People; who were none of his Disciples, nor had any regard for him. Supposing he could, by his divine Power infuse a Pannick [=**panic**] Fear into the People; yet what was the Reason, that he was so eaten up with zeal against the Profanation of that House, which he himself came to destroy, and which he permitted, I may say commanded to be filthily polluted not long after.[1]

Commentary. This statement is rather odd and Woolston's context does not help us alleviate the difficulties with it. Throughout the book how to take Woolston's vision of Jesus in light of his allegorical exegesis is very odd, and this statement is what makes it all the more so. The indication here from "It is hard to conceive, how any one in the Form of a Man, and a despised one too, [...] with a Whip in his Hand could execute such a Work upon a great Multitude of People" may imply that Woolston did not think Jesus incarnated or that he could not have been a human person. Indeed, this statement seems to imply it enough that other commentators have argued that he is, indeed, casting doubts on the historicity of Christ, as Herrick notes.[2] Of course, it is impossible to tell in full, however, I am inclined to agree with Herrick on this, in that we have here another figure who is implicitly casting doubt on the historicity of Jesus, to do so in full would be to incur the wrath of even more censors and authorities, which Woolston was already the enemy of, living out his last years in a prison cell because of his challenges to orthodoxic Christian views.

---

[1] Thomas Woolston, *A Fourth Discourse on the Miracles of Our Saviour* (London: 1728), 22.

[2] James Herrick, "Blasphemy in the Eighteenth Century: Contours of a Rhetorical Crime," in Wayne Hudson, Diego Lucci, and Jeffrey Wigelsworth (eds), *Atheism and Deism Revalued: Heterodox Religious Identities in Britain, 1650-1800* (Surrey: Ashgate, 2014), p. 106.

François-Marie Arouet (1694-1778), better known as "Voltaire", is one of the most noted figures in this debate primarily because he records a group of deists who followed the work of one Lord Bolingbroke (presumably this is Henry St. John, 1st Viscount Bolingbroke, 1678-1751) and who argued emphatically and in no unambiguous language that Jesus did not exist.

Relevant Passage.

I saw some disciples of Bolingbroke, more ingenious than educated, who denied the existence of Jesus because the story of the three wise men and the star and the massacre of the innocents are, they said, the height of eccentricity; the contradiction of the two genealogies that Matthew and Luke gave is especially a reason that these young men allege to persuade themselves that there was no Jesus. But they drew a very false conclusion.[1]

Commentary. Voltaire is emphatic here that these figures (unnamed) regarded Jesus to be an ahistorical figure. The argument that Voltaire reports them as having, however, is rather peculiar. Here, they seem to have come to the conclusion that Jesus did not exist based on the fact that the genealogies given in the gospels of Matthew and Luke are in contradiction with themselves. One can only infer that

---

[1] Translation from Voltaire, *God and Human Beings*, translated by Michael Shreve (Amherst: Prometheus Books, 2010), Kindle Edition, location 1009. Originally found in Voltaire, *Oeuvres complètes de Voltaire*, vol. xxxiii (Paris: Société Littéraire-Typographique, 1785).

following from this, since the text was proven to be contradictory that they then argued the whole of the New Testament could, therefore, not be trusted to provide historical information that is reliable. However, this is speculation and it is unfortunately uncertain what all went into their thesis. Voltaire responds at length by arguing that Josephus' *Testimonium Flavianum* (*Antiquities* 18.3.3) was not a wholesale forgery and also pointed out that on standards of evidence, the tales of Pythagoras have just as much eccentric and problematic material as well, so why not also doubt him. It is worth noting how this does parallel to quite a degree the work of Stillingfleet, some ninety-two years earlier.

This particular passage is noteworthy since it is the only one which has been cited as a pre-Volney passage with any regularity in the literature on the historicity of Jesus (with the exception of Meggitt and Goguel).[2] As such, it is somewhat more well-known, but not to a high extent, still being ignored by academics such as Ehrman in his own historiographical overview of the debate.[3]

---

[2] Archibald Robertson, *Jesus: Myth or History?* (London: Watts & Co., 1946), 41; Robert van Voorst, *Jesus Outside the New Testament: An Introduction to the Ancient Evidence* (Grand Rapids: Eerdmans, 2000), 8.
[3] Bart Ehrman, *Did Jesus Exist? The Historical Argument for Jesus of Nazareth* (New York: HarperOne, 2012), 14-19.

There are a number of smaller comments that can be found in writings from the early 1700's up to the time of Volney's writings, though most unfortunately elude any heavy description of who they are in reference to or where they come from. In this chapter I will compile these as much as possible and enable readers to see what some of our surviving documentation on Jesus Skepticism actually looks like.

4) Robert Jenkin (1698)

"That in the reign of Tiberius there lived such a person as Jesus Christ, who suffered (a) under Pontius Pilate, is expressly written by Tacitus: and that he cured Diseases and wrought other Miracles, was never denied by the worst Enemies to the Christian Name and Doctrine."[1]

Commentary. This is the second oldest statement we have in defense of the historicity of Jesus, once again (as with Stillingfleet) making exceptional use of Tacitus for this defense. No figures are named as the target of this, but it is implicit that there would be someone that Jenkin was familiar with who made such doubts public to him, otherwise he would not see such a need as to defend that Christ actually lived.

5) Hugo Grotius (1627)

"That there was such a Person as *Jesus* of *Nazareth*, who lived heretofore in *Judea*, when *Tiberius* was Emperour of *Rome*, is not only

---

[1] Robert Jenkin, *The Reasonableness and Certainty of the Christian Religion*, Vol. 1 (London: Peter Buck, 1698), 257.

most constantly professed by all Christians,
who are scattered over the face of all the Earth:
but acknowledged by all the *Jews*, who now
are, or ever wrote since those times. Nay, the
very *Pagan* Writers, that is, such as are neither
of *Jewish* nor *Christian Religion*, namely,
Suetonius, *Tacitus*, *Pliny* the Younger, and
many more after them do testifie [=**testify**] the
same."[2]

Commentary. In this small section, we have an affirmation of
the historicity of Jesus, relying on the typical pagan authors
that are seen often referenced in today's literature on the
existence of Christ. Grotius, here, affirms this likely in
response to well known allegations that Christ did not exist.
This is one of the earliest known defenses of Jesus' historicity.

6) Laurent Francois (writing in 1754)

Fr. "*vous ne pouvez non plus croire que ceux
qui nous assurent de l'existence de Jesus
Christ, de ses miracles, des livres du nouveau
Testament, aient été dans l'erreur sur tous ces
fait, sans la faire retomber sur Dieu même.*"[3]

Eng. "You cannot still believe that those who
assure us of the existence of Jesus Christ, his
miracles, the books of the New Testament were

---

[2] Hugo Grotius, *The Truth of Christian Religion: In six Books. Written in
Latin and Now Translated into English with the Addition of a Seventh Book
Against the present Roman Church*, trans. Simon Patrick (London: J. L.,
1700), Book 2 page 40. Originally translated from *De veritate religionis
Christianae* (1627).

[3] Laurent Francois, *Preuves de la Religion de Jesus-Christ, contre les
Spinosistes et les Deistes*, vol. 3 (Paris, 1754), 564.

errant on all of these facts, without making it
fall onto God himself."

Commentary. This reference is far clearer for interpretation
than that of Valla. In this case, Francois seems to be directly
complaining from his own knowledge about a group of people
who deny that Jesus ever existed and that the New Testament
was errant. Unfortunately, we are not given any detailed
information about their arguments, who they are, or where
they come from. The text we merely know is in response to
deists and other non-believers who were critics of the Bible.

7) **An Encyclopedia Affirmation of Existence (1757)**

Fr. *"La certitude que nous avons que les
dogmas que nous croyons sont révélés, est dans
le genre moral. Les élémens de cette certitude
sont des faits, des motifs de crédibilité, &c. Or
ces faits, ces motifs. &c. l'existence de Jesus-
Christ qui a apporté aux hommes la revelation,
sa vie, ses miracles, toutes les preuves de la
verité & des livres saints, & de la divinité de la
religion chrétienne; tout cela est dans le genre
moral."*[4]

Eng. "The certainty that we have that the
dogmas we believe are revealed is in the moral
genre. The elements of this certainty are facts,
motives of credibility, etc. Now these facts,
these motives, etc. The existence of Jesus
Christ, who brought to men the revelation, his
life, his miracles, all the proofs of the truth and

---

[4] Société des Gens de Lettres, *Encyclopedie ou Dictionnaire Raisonné*, vol.
vii (Paris, 1757), 18.

of the holy books, and of the divinity of the Christian religion; all this is in the moral genre."

Commentary. Here, we do not have reference to Jesus Skeptics, however it is stated that it is a matter of fact that Jesus, himself, existed. This does seem to insinuate, possibly, that there were some who doubted that he did live, which we know from (1) that, yes, there did seem to be those who had such doubts in mind when they publicly argued against the Christian faith. The importance of this is that it is contemporary with (1) and so we can at least use these two to help situate our context and thinking about this passage. Both are French, they are three years apart, and are both discussing whether Jesus ever lived. Thus, there is some reason to at least consider placing them in a single context together.

8) **William Cayley (1759)**

"There are People who deny the truth of this whole account, who assert that no such divine person ever made his appearance in the world. In this place I shall only observe, that if the concurrent testimony of a great number of credible and competent witnesses be sufficient to establish the truth of any historical fact; if to fulfill prophecies, to work the most amazing miracles, and that in confirmation of the purest doctrine, be genuine marks of divinity; and, lastly, if it be impossible for the benevolent Creator to impose upon his creatures, then may we boldly pronounce the above assertion to be false.

But they go further, and pretend to assign a reason to their unbelief; God, say they, is infinitely wise, and by consequence can never be supposed to act but for a wise end; man was created a rational creature, endued with the faculties to discover his Creator, with understanding to investigate, and with power to obey his will: and they add, that happiness, no doubt, would be the consequence of such obedience: what need then of a new revelation from heaven? What need then of a new method of salvation thro' [=through] the merits of Jesus Christ?

Here then is another foundation laid, and that mentioned in my text entirely set aside: for if this reasoning be just, either Christ never lived; or if He did, He lived and died in vain, and not on Him, but on our own obedience, must we found our hopes of future happiness."[5]

Commentary. In this longer passage we do not have much information except that there seemed to be a group of figures who denied the existence of Christ as coming in the flesh and offering salvation, instead arguing that true happiness, if knowledge and intelligence were afforded to man by God, would then allow them to attain future happiness and therefore the salvation of Christ was unnecessary. Thus, either Christ never came and existed at all, or if he did, he did so in vain.

9) **Johann Gottlieb Töllner (1764)**

Ger. *"Freund, du bist am Rande der unvernünstigsten zweifelsucht, wenn du nichts weiteres, und bestimteres für Dich hast, als*

---

[5] William Cayley, *A Sermon, Preached in the Cathedral Church of York, on Sunday the 4th Day of March, 1759* (York: Caesar Ward, 1759), 7-8.

daß, es an sich möglich ist, daß Jesus nie gelebt, oder doch nie das gelehrt und gethan habe, was die Evangelisten vor ihm berichten."[6]

Eng: *"Friend, you are on the brink of unreasonable skepticism if you have nothing further and more certain for yourself than that it is possible that Jesus never lived, or never taught and did what the Gospels ascribe him."*

Commentary. This reference is rather intriguing in that Töllner is responding to an unnamed "freund" here but records at least something about what this figure seemed to suggest. In a bought of skepticism, this enigmatic character seems to have made the arguments that either Jesus may have not existed or if he did nothing in the Gospels ascribed to him was accurate or true. The reference comes roughly contemporary with the previous two we have seen, and is also just two years before the followers of Bolingbroke would be discussed by Voltaire, thus, by this time we may be inclined to think that there was at least a developing underground of critics who argued that Jesus may have never existed at all. I am, somewhat, inclined to see this, given how long we have seen this criticism pointed out by a number of figures from this timeframe, and its general location among deists who critiqued Christianity.

---

[6] Johann Gottlieb Töllner, *Wahre Gründe warum Gott die Offenbarung nicht mit augenscheinlichern Beweisen versehn hat*, band 1 (Waysenhaus- und Frommannische Handlung, 1764), 201.

There are a number of comments which are, unfortunately, questionable as to what they are fully attempting to entail. Comments of these type tend to be rather enigmatic and short, without the ability for context to alleviate our struggles to understand them. As such, we are only left with the comments as they stand. Thus, here I will compile them and attempt to give commentary where it can be applicable, otherwise there will be little and just short notes.

10) Laurentius Valla (ref. 1697)

Valla, a 15th century Catholic priest and commentator who is reported as stating:

> Fr. "*qu'il y avait des flèches dans son carquois contre le Messie lui-même.*"[1]

> Eng. "that there were in his quiver arrows against the Messiah himself"

Commentary. Unfortunately, the nature of this phrase is uncertain. It is only recorded in the *Dictionary of Historical Criticism* (1697) by Pierre Bayle, and as such it dates 240 years after the speaker, without any antecedent evidence of its authenticity. As such, it is hard to say whether this is, at all, an accurate reflection of something that Valla would have said. It must also be noted, for sake of completion, that it could also be a polemical phrase put in his mouth (see chapter on *Polemics*).

---

[1] Pierre Bayle, *Dictionaire historique et critique*, vol. XIV (Doseor, 1820), 321 (originally printed in 1697).

However, if we assumed authenticity for the sake of argument, we have another critical issue: that of not knowing precisely what this entails. Does this mean that he has evidence against the Messiah (Jesus) ever existing, against his divinity, against his miracles, etc.? Ultimately, without context, we are in an epistemological dead zone. However, the reference still belongs in this uncertain category. If this could be confirmed to be authentic and a reference to Jesus Skepticism, however, it would be the earliest on record.

11) On Mani (ref. 1762)

"He [Mani, text calls "Manes"] taught the doctrine sate and necessity, denied the existence of Christ in the flesh, with innumerable other false and fantastic notions, which may be found by those, who shall think it worth their while to seek for them, in Epiphanius Adversus haereses."[2]

Commentary. In this passage, it is unclear the text is attempting to discuss the heresy of Docetism, which the entry does not name on this issue, or whether it may be insinuating the idea that Mani actually rejected an earthly presence for Jesus. The phrase "denied the existence of Christ in the flesh" is uncertain, unfortunately. Of course, this is questionable and while the author cites Epiphanius here, it is curious that Manichaeism frequently upheld Jesus as having a human mother.[3] Thus, we must also consider that this might be a late polemic.

---

[2] Numerous, *A New and General Biographical Dictionary*, vol. viii (London: Printed for Various Persons, 1762), 205.
[3] Werner Sundermann, "CHRISTIANITY v. Christ in Manicheism," in *Encyclopædia Iranica*, vol. V, fasc. 5 (Costa Mesa, 1991), 335-39.

There are a number of references which are, most likely, all examples of polemics being used in an attempt to discredit various different opponents. Jesus Skepticism appears to have been used by Christians often to polemicize various different sects of Christianity, for example, Quakers. Here we can demonstrate a number of examples of this.

12) **John Bale (1574)**

"'All ages can testify enough how profitable that fable of Christ has been to us and our companies.'"[1]

Commentary. This text is particularly perplexing because it comes to us from a text by one John Bale (1495-1563), who was a public opponent of the Catholic Church and often known for polemicizing them with impunity. This text in particular comes to us from his *The Pageant of Popes* (1574) and was a statement put in the mouth of Pope Leo X (1475-1521). Unfortunately, there are two major issues with it. (1) The passage is vague, and we do not know what the statement "fable of Christ" fully entails, and context does not alleviate this issue. (2) The text is polemical, so whether or not this is authentic and actually goes back to Leo X is in such extreme doubt that it renders this particularly problematic. Even if we assumed authenticity, however, the problems in (1) would still prohibit us from making much of it. However, I include it hear because it was interpreted by subsequent mythicists to be a statement of the ahistoricity of Christ.[2] As such, it is considered a polemical reference.

---

[1] John Bale, *The Pageant of Popes*, translated into English (London: T. Marshe, 1574), fol. 179, 228 see under "163. Leo the Tenth."
[2] Robert Taylor, *The Diegesis* (Boston: J. P. Mendum, 1853), p. 35n*;

13) Johannes Lorenz von Mosheim (1724)

"The European Quakers dare not so far presume upon the indulgence of the civil and ecclesiastical powers, as to deny openly, the reality of the history of the life, meditation, and sufferings of Christ; but in America, where they have nothing to fear, they are said to express themselves, without ambiguity, on this subject, and to maintain publicly, that Christ never existed but in the hearts of the faithful. This point was debated between Keith and his adversaries in several general assemblies of the sect, held in England, and was at length brought before the parliament. The contest was terminated, in the year 1695, by the excommunication of Keith and his adherents, which so exasperated this famous Quaker, that he returned some year after this, into the bosom of the English church, and died in its communion."[3]

Commentary. This text is clearly a polemic against the Quakers, specifically targeting George Keith (1638-1716) as arguing that Jesus never existed, especially also other Quakers in America. This entire segment has no backing from other historical sources and, in fact, the translator (Archibald MacLaine) provided a note [Y] at the bottom of the page, specifically on the authority of one Bishop Burnet, that von

Minas Papageorgiou, *Jesus Mythicism: An Introduction*, translated by Rania Ioannou (Thessaloniki: iWrite.gr Publications, 2015), ebook, position, 327-344.

[3] I use here the translation from Johannes Lorenz von Mosheim, *An Ecclesiastical History*, translated by Archibald MacLaine, vol. 2 (London: A. Millar, 1765), 537.

Mosheim's records seemed to be inaccurate and that Keith had, instead, left because he had become frustrated that the American Quakers were more akin to "deists" than what he wished, and his opposition led the Quakers themselves to sending him back to England. Thus, even not long after von Mosheim wrote this passage, its accuracy was already being called into doubt, and there are no records I have found from Keith's writings that would at all insinuate that he was, in fact, ever rejecting the historical life of Christ.

14) Unknown Author (1766)

"The self-same evidence, which informs us, that any such persons as Jesus and his apostles ever existed, informs us likewise, that the supernatural doctrines of the New Testament itself, were just as truly their doctrines, as the moral."[4]

Commentary. This was written in *The Monthly Review or Literary Journal* in 1766. The text itself is not a direct reference to Jesus Skeptics, in that it is a quote from an author that was being reviewed, who was responding in turn to someone else. The listed writings are *A Defence of Revelation in general* by an unknown "Rational Christian" who is rebutting to a work by unknown opponents entitled *The Morality of the New Testament*. In context, this work apparently argued that *only* the moral writings in the New Testament could actually be considered historical, while the rest was forged and interpolated, in effect, a massive patchwork series (akin to the Dutch Radicals with the epistles[5])

---

[4] *The Monthly Review or Literary Journal* 35 (London: R. Griffiths, 1766), 131.

[5] Thomas Whittaker, *The Origins of Christianity with An Outline of Van Manen's Analysis of the Pauline Literature* (London: Watts & Co., 1904);

. Here, the author of *A Defence* attempts to create a counterargument that there is no reason to consider any element an interpolation over another, by using Jesus and the apostles' existences as the linchpin. As such, here we can see how skepticism of Jesus' existence was actually used as a counter argument meant to discredit other people's positions.

15) **Forged Pope Paul III Reference (1846)**

"[Pope Paul III] carried impiety to the point of affirming that Christ was none other than the sun worshiped by the Mithraic sect represented in paganism. He explained the allegories of his incarnation and resurrection by the parallel between Christ and Mithras. His counterargument was that the constellation Virgo, or better said of Isis, corresponding to the solstice and prevailing at the birth of Mithras, had been adopted as a metaphor for the birth of Jesus, who, according to the Pope, was adequate evidence that Jesus and Mithras were the same god. He dared to say that there was no proof, no unquestionable authenticity, which would be enough to prove that Jesus was ever a historical person and, therefore, he himself believed that Jesus never existed."[6]

G. A. van den Bergh van Eysinga, *Radical Views About the New Testament*, trans. S. B. Black (London: Watts & Co., 1912); Hermann Detering, *The Fabricated Paul: Early Christianity in the Twilight*, trans. Darrell Doughty (Dusseldorf: Patmos Press, 2003 and 2018); Robert M. Price, *The Amazing Colossal Apostle: The Search for the Historical Paul* (Salt Lake City: Signature Books, 2012) and (as ed.), *A Wave of Hypercriticism: The English Writings of W. C. van Manen* (Valley: Tellectual Press, 2013-2014).

[6] Papageorgiou, 2015, location 318-336.

Commentary. In this passage we are informed that Pope Paul III (1468-1549) apparently claimed that Jesus was a sun myth, based on Mithras and associated with the constellations. There are a number of huge problems in using this text however, which prevent me from giving it much credence, and have prevented it from gaining traction in other historiographical work as well.

The first major issue is the date. There is no copy of this manuscript with dates before the work of Louis Marie de Cormenin (1788-1868).[7] This is where all information, including Guy Fau (whom Papageorgiou cites) stems from. Which means we ultimately have no way to establish any providence of this before the 1800's. While de Cormenin does claim that this text he portrays is based on a report from one Diego Hurtado de Mendoza (1503-1575), however, there is no citation of what manuscript, letter, or anything else that it comes from in de Cormenin's work, and I have been unable to find anything which precedes de Cormenin on this. As such, we have reason from a text perspective to consider that this is not an authentic statement going back to Pope Paul III.

Secondly, everything that is placed in the mouth of Pope Paul III here is extremely doubtful given that it bears remarkable resemblance to the works of Volney and Dupuis.[8] These were written before de Cormenin's own work, and given that de Cormenin was a French scholar and wrote some time after Volney and Dupuis had published, we have much reason to suspect that he would be familiar with their works. Thus, we have content reasons to think that this is not authentic either.

---

[7] Louis Marie de Cormenin, *The Public and Private History of The Popes of Rome*, translated from French, vol. 1 (Philadelphia: T. B. Peterson, 1846), 203.

[8] G. A. Wells, "Stages of New Testament Criticism," *Journal of the History of Ideas* 30 (1969): 147-160.

From these two perspectives, I am inclined to think that this is a polemic, as the translator of the work (see the unpaginated translator's preface) complained, against the Catholic Church, and that de Cormenin was specifically inventing a mythicist statement using the works of Volney and (or) Dupuis.

APPENDIX: SUPPOSED ANCIENT SOURCES

There fact remains that there is, in reality, little to nothing that would explicitly in any manner suggest a mythological Jesus in any way in ancient writings. Georges Ory had attempted at one time to bring people's attention to a late Greek Magical Papyri—PGM IV:1230-1235, 3020— however the text dates so late that it is, in reality unusable for any argumentation. We would already expect by the fourth century CE that Jesus would have been celestial in nature, furthermore, the text does not indicate that this was his only place. The "conjuring" mentioned in the text is of little consequence given the late date.[1]

Another text which has been occasionally brought to the attention of historicists is the *Historia Augusta*, which has a letter (purportedly written by Hadrian) wherein it mentions that in Egypt there were "Christians" who worshiped "Serapis" as Christ. The passage reads:

> From Hadrian Augustus to Servianus the consul, greeting. The land of Egypt, the praises of which you have been recounting to me, my dear Servianus, I have found to be wholly light-minded, unstable, and blown about by every breath of rumour. There those who worship Serapis are, in fact, Christians, and those who call themselves bishops of Christ are, in fact, devotees of Serapis. There is no chief of the Jewish synagogue, no Samaritan, no Christian presbyter, who is not an astrologer, a

---

[1] Hans Dieter Betz (ed.), *The Greek Magical Papyri in Translation including the Demotic Spells* (Chicago: University of Chicago Press, 1986), XXIII, 62, 96. For another spell that mentions Jesus, see PGM CXXVIII.1-11, *The Greek Magical Papyri*, 323.

soothsayer, or an anointer. Even the Patriarch himself, when he comes to Egypt, is forced by some to worship Serapis, by others to worship Christ.[2]

The text, however, is likely a late forgery and, once again, as a result it does not indicate what earliest Christians believed.[3] In fact, even if written by Hadrian it would still be too late to make anything of it (as he was writing in the second century). Thus, this letter is of no help to us in attempting to establish any ancient Christians who regarded Jesus as a purely mythological figure.

As we have seen from our investigation, the earlier first and second century writings which we can confirm are more likely to come from that era do not regard Jesus as a purely celestial being. Jewish and pagan writings simply are not concerned with any mythological Jesus. The exception to this which has been argued for has been in Justin Martyr's *Dialogue with Trypho*, where the (possibly fictional) character of Trypho makes the following statement:

> But the Christ, if he has indeed been born, and exists anywhere, is unknown, and doesn't even yet know himself, and has no power until Elijah comes to anoint him, and make him appear to all. But you, on the basis of groundless hearsay, invent a Christ for yourselves, and for this sake you are now irresponsibly doomed.[4]

---

[2] *Historia Augusta*, "And Bonosus" VIII, 399-401.

[3] Alan Cameron, *The Last Pagans of Rome* (Oxford: Oxford University Press, 2010), 743-746.

[4] From Richard Carrier, *On the Historicity of Jesus: Why We Might Have Reason for Doubt* (Sheffield: Sheffield Phoenix Press, 2014), 350.

There have been two lines of argumentation to trying to argue that this statement indicates a mythological Jesus was believed. Earlier mythicists attempted to try and eliminate the contextual phrase after "unknown" from the passage when referring to it, thus making it seem to readers that the passage was purely mythological in nature.[5] This is no longer entertained, however, as historicists were quick to catch on to this sleight of hand. Instead, now there are attempts to simply treat the passage as mythological, despite the fact that the contextual phrase of "and doesn't even yet know himself, and has no power until Elijah comes to anoint him" clearly indicates that Trypho is taking the Christian Christ as historical, he just does not think he is the Christ because he has not been anointed by Elijah, thus he cannot even know who he is. Furthermore, it makes no sense for this fictional dialogue[6] invented by Justin to use such an argument, especially since Justin never counters it. Instead, his counter argument is that Jesus *is* the Christ.[7] Furthermore, throughout the rest of the *Dialogue*, Trypho always refers to Jesus as historical.[8] While Price has made the argument that Trypho is merely made to have these arguments by Justin, it would make no contextual sense for Justin to do that in every single other location, but leave this one open.[9] Thus, the mythicist arguments for Trypho attesting to a mythological Jesus or a charge that Jesus did not exist do not hold up to scrutiny. There is no contextual reason why Justin would give Trypho such an argument here, but then never follow up on it and

---

[5] This was the tactic of L. Gordon Rylands and J. M. Robertson.

[6] Robertson, *Jesus: Myth or History?* 25.

[7] Robertson, *Jesus: Myth or History?* 25-26.

[8] Michael Slusser (ed), *St. Justin Martyr: Dialogue with Trypho* (Washington DC: The Catholic University of America Press, 2003), 48-49, 56, 61, 73-74, 103.

[9] Robert M. Price, *Bart Ehrman Interpreted: How One Radical New Testament Scholar Understands Another* (Durham: Pitchstone Publishing, 2018), 66-67.

make this Jewish opponent then regard Jesus as historical for the rest of the debate. It is completely incoherent. Justin is the inventor of this entire *Dialogue*, and it is even possible that Trypho is just a figment.[10] There is no reason to take this passage in any way as pro-mythicist.

Another passage which has had surprisingly little discussion is a mention in the Sibylline Oracles of an apparently apocalyptic return of the Hebrew Joshua, which one would think mythicists would have used at some point to argue for an ahistorical Jesus in more detail. The passage reads:

> And one shall come again from heaven, a man
> Preeminent, whose hands on fruitful tree
> By far the noblest of the Hebrews stretched,
> Who at one time did make the sun stand still[11]

The reasons why this passage has not been used become apparent if one reads the rest of the work. It does not appear Christian in origin. So, the fact that there is this odd Christianized identification of Joshua with Jesus here makes one suspicious. The passage's integrity is of a dubious nature and very likely it is of an interpolated origin. As such, it is of *later* than written date (the whole of book V being written around 80-90 CE). Thus, it does not indicate anything about the historicity of Jesus or how he was perceived in earliest Christianity for us.[12] A similar problem is that of the *Apocalypse of Ezra*.[13] We still have no evidence yet of any mythological conceptions of Jesus, then.

---

[10] Claudia Setzer, *Jewish Responses to Early Christians* (Minneapolis: Fortress Press, 1994), 215.

[11] Milton S. Terry, *The Sibylline Oracles: Translated from the Greek into English Blank Verse* (1899), 128.

[12] Stephen Felder, "What is 'The Fifth Sibylline Oracle'?" *Journal for the Study of Judaism in the Persian, Hellenistic, and Roman Period* 33, no. 4 (2002): 363-385.

Carrier and Price argue that 2 Peter responds to a group of Christians who thought that the stories of Jesus were simply myths and that it provides direct evidence of a transition from Jesus mysteries to a historical orthodoxy.[14] Unfortunately, 2 Peter 1-2 says no such thing. The reference to "cleverly devised stories" in 1:16 cannot be construed to mean that Jesus as a person was a myth. This passage easily could refer to his birth, to his transfiguration, or to his resurrection, the second of which is directly referenced in the following verse, 1:17, or (more generally) just the supernatural stories (μῦθος) of Jesus in general and not have anything to do with the historicity of the figure. Carrier's translation of μῦθος as "fable" is also questionable, since μῦθος refers to any kind of story, fictional or historical, there was not a particular differentiation. As such, "cleverly devised stories," is preferred over the translation Carrier gives, which seems to presuppose his mythicist interpretation. In fact, I would challenge Carrier or any mythicist to find an example where μῦθος is in an exclusively mythical fashion in regard to a figure. 2 Peter 2 also does not lend credence to Carrier's reading additionally because the context is that it is talking of False Prophets who have led people astray due to false prophecy teaching (see 2 Peter 1:19-2:3). Carrier's reading is simply a projection of his presuppositions upon the text, which simply does not indicate this to be the case. There is nothing to clearly indicate this epistle talks of any mythic-Christ worshipers. Carrier's reading of this pseudepigraphic epistle is

---

[13] Archibald Robertson, *The Origins of Christianity*, Revised Edition (New York: International Publishers, 1962), 73 argues that this indicates that Jewish people wished for Joshua to return. However, more recent scholarship suggests that the apocalypse has been entirely reworked or even written by Christians, see James Charlesworth, *The Pseudepigrapha and Modern Research, With a Supplement* (Atlanta: Scholars Press, 1981), 116-117 (citation courtesy of *EarlyChristianWritings.com*).

[14] Carrier, *On the Historicity of Jesus*, 351 and Price, *Bart Ehrman Interpreted*, 67.

simply ad hoc. The same problems pervade Price's own reading. There is simply no reason to take this as indicating Christians worshiped a mythological Christ, as such a reading is undermined by the sheer context of the passage.

This rather well establishes that there is no reason to consider there as having been ancient evidence for mythicism. Most of Carrier's (and company) other references, such as Philo or the Ascension of Isaiah are speculative and have been dealt with elsewhere.[15] As such, I do not include them as particularly pertinent or valuable here. These appear to be cases of unjustified and problematic interpretations of the sources, rather than a case of having any ancient evidence which would support the notion of mythicism. As such, it is to be dismissed until further evaluation.

---

[15] Larry Hurtado, "Gee, Dr. Carrier, You're Really Upset!" *Larry Hurtado's Blog* (2017), larryhurtado.wordpress.com/2017/12/07/gee-dr-carrier-youre-really-upset/; Daniel N. Gullotta, "On Richard Carrier's Doubts: A Response to Richard Carrier's 'On the Historicity of Jesus: Why We Might Have Reason for Doubt'," *Journal for the Study of the Historical Jesus* 15 (2017): 310-346; M. David Litwa, *How the Gospels Became History* (New Haven: Yale University Press, 2019), 22-45.

Included here is a complete bibliography of works cited throughout for ease of finding, for those who find footnotes tedious or difficult to wade through. This includes all primary and secondary literature.

Primary Sources (Ancient with/out Translations)

Bietz, Hans Dieter.
1986   [as editor] *The Greek Magical Papyri in Translation including the Demotic Spells* (Chicago: University of Chicago Press)

Historia Augusta.
4th-5th C. CE   "And Bonosus" VIII, 399-401.

Josephus.
93-94 CE   *Antiquities of the Jews* 18.3.3

Slusser, Michael.
2003   [as editor] *St. Justin Martyr: Dialogue with Trypho* (Washington DC: The Catholic University of America Press)

Tacitus.
115 CE   *Annals* 15.44

Terry, Milton S.
1899   *The Sibylline Oracles: Translated from the Greek into English Blank Verse* (1899)

Primary Sources (Main Text).

Anonymous.

1712   "Historical and Critical Reflections on Mahometanism and Socinianism," in *Four Treatises concerning the Doctrine, Discipline and Worship of the Mahometans* (London: B. Lintott), 196-197

Bale, John.
1574   *The Pageant of Popes*, translated into English (London: T. Marshe)

Bayle, Pierre.
1697/1820   *Dictionaire historique et critique*, vol. XIV (Doseor)

Cayley, William.
1759   *A Sermon, Preached in the Cathedral Church of York, on Sunday the 4th Day of March, 1759* (York: Caesar Ward)

De Cormenin, Louis Marie.
1846   *The Public and Private History of The Popes of Rome*, translated from French, vol. 1 (Philadelphia: T. B. Peterson)

Francois, Laurent.
1754   *Preuves de la Religion de Jesus-Christ, contre les Spinosistes et les Deistes*, vol. 3 (Paris)

Grotius, Hugo.
1700   *The Truth of Christian Religion: In six Books. Written in Latin and Now Translated into English with the Addition of a Seventh Book Against the present Roman Church*, trans. Simon Patrick (London: J. L., 1700), Book 2

page 40. Originally translated from *De veritate religionis Christianae* (1627).

Hardouin, Jean.

1729   Jean Hardouin (au.) and Hermann Detering (ed.), *Prolegomena*, trans. Edwin Johnson (Independently Published, trans. ed. repri. 2017)

Jenkin, Robert.

1698   *The Reasonableness and Certainty of the Christian Religion*, Vol. 1 (London: Peter Buck, 1698)

More, Henry.

1660   *An Explanation of the Grand Mystery of Godliness: Or, A True and Faithfull Representation of the Everlasting Gospel of Our Lord and Saviour Jesus Christ, the Onely Begotten Son of God and Sovereign Over Men and Angels* (London: F. Flesher)

Von Mosheim, Johannes Lorenz.

1765   *An Ecclesiastical History*, translated by Archibald MacLaine, vol. 2 (London: A. Millar)

Numerous.

1762   *A New and General Biographical Dictionary*, vol. viii (London: Printed for Various Persons)

Société des Gens de Lettres

1757   *Encyclopedie ou Dictionnaire Raisonné*, vol. vii (Paris)

Stillingfleet, Edward.

1677   *A Letter to a Deist, in Answer to Several Objections against the Truth and Authority of the Scriptures* (London: W. G.)

Töllner, Johann Gottlieb.
1764   *Wahre Gründe warum Gott die Offenbarung nicht mit augenscheinlichern Beweisen versehn hat*, band 1 (Waysenhaus und Frommannische Handlung)

Unknown.
1766   *The Monthly Review or Literary Journal* 35 (London: R. Griffiths), 131

Voltaire.
2010   *God and Human Beings*, translated by Michael Shreve (Amherst: Prometheus Books), Kindle Edition

1785   *Oeuvres complètes de Voltaire*, vol. xxxiii (Paris: Société Littéraire-Typographique)

Woolston, Thomas.
1728   *A Fourth Discourse on the Miracles of Our Saviour* (London)

Secondary Sources.

Van den Bergh van Eysinga, G. A.
1912   *Radical Views About the New Testament*, trans. S. B. Black (London: Watts & Co.)

Blom, Willem.

2019   "Why the Testimonium Taciteum Is Authentic: A Response to Carrier," *Vigiliae Christianae* 73, no. 5: 564-581

Byrne, James Malcolm.
1998   *Religion and the Enlightenment: From Descartes to Kant* (Louisville: Westminster John Knox Press)

Cameron, Alan.
2010   *The Last Pagans of Rome* (Oxford: Oxford University Press)

Carrier, Richard.
2014   "The Prospect of a Christian Interpolation in Tacitus, *Annals* 15:44," *Vigilae Christianae* 68: 1-20

     On the Historicity of Jesus: Why We Might Have Reason for Doubt (Sheffield: Sheffield Phoenix Press)

Charlesworth, James.
1981   *The Pseudepigrapha and Modern Research, With a Supplement* (Atlanta: Scholars Press)

Detering, Hermann.
2017   *Inszenierte Fälschungen: Die Paulusbriefe in der holländischen Radikalkritik* (Independently Published)

2003, 2018 *The Fabricated Paul: Early Christianity in the Twilight*, trans. Darrell Doughty (Dusseldorf: Patmos Press)

Drews, Arthur.
1926   *Die Leugnung der Geschichtlichkeit Jesu in Vergangenheit und Gegenwart* (Karlsruhe)

Ehrman, Bart.
2012   *Did Jesus Exist? The Historical Argument for Jesus of Nazareth* (New York: HarperOne)

Evans, Craig.
1994   "Jesus in Non-Christian Sources," in Bruce Chilton and Craig A. Evans (eds.), *Studying the Historical Jesus: Evaluations of the State of Current Research* (Leiden: Brill), 443-478

Felder, Stephen.
2002   "What is 'The Fifth Sibylline Oracle'?" *Journal for the Study of Judaism in the Persian, Hellenistic, and Roman Period* 33, no. 4: 363-385

Gullotta, Daniel N.
2017   "On Richard Carrier's Doubts: A Response to Richard Carrier's 'On the Historicity of Jesus: Why We Might Have Reason for Doubt'," *Journal for the Study of the Historical Jesus* 15: 310-346

Herrick, James.
2014   "Blasphemy in the Eighteenth Century: Contours of a Rhetorical Crime," in Wayne Hudson, Diego Lucci, and Jeffrey Wigelsworth (eds), *Atheism and Deism Revalued: Heterodox Religious Identities in Britain, 1650-1800* (Surrey: Ashgate), 101-118

Jongeneel, Jan A. B.
2009   *Jesus Christ in World History* (Frankfurt am Main: Peter Lang)

Kryvelev, Iosif A.
1987   *Christ: Myth or Reality?* "Religious Studies in the USSR" Series (Moscow: USSR Academy of Sciences and "Social Sciences Today" Editorial Board, 1987)

Lataster, Raphael.
2019   *Questioning the Historicity of Jesus: Why a Philosophical Analysis Elucidates the Historical Discourse* (Leiden: Brill | Rodopi)

Lenzman, Y. A.
1967   "Izucheniye sovetskimi uchenymi rannego khristianstva," *Voprosy nauchnogo ateizma* 4: 284

Litwa, M. David.
2019   *How the Gospels Became History* (New Haven: Yale University Press)

McClymond, Michael.
2004   *Familiar Stranger: An Introduction to Jesus of Nazareth* (Grand Rapids: Eerdmans)

Meggitt, Justin.
2019   "'More Ingenious Than Learned'? Examining the Quest for the Non-Historical Jesus," *New Testament Studies* 65: 443-460

2017   "Was the Historical Jesus an Anarchist?" in A. Christoyannopoulos and M. S. Adams, *Essays in Anarchism and Religion: Volume 1* (Stockholm: Stockholm University Press), 124-197

Papageorgiou, Minas.

2015   *Jesus Mythicism: An Introduction*, translated by Rania Ioannou (Thessaloniki: iWrite.gr Publications), ebook

Papoušek, Dalibor.

2001   "The Soviet School of Historians of Early Christianity and Its Influence in Former Czechoslovakia: The Question of Jesus' Historicity," in Iva Doležalová, Luther H. Martin and Dalibor Papoušek (eds.), *The Academic Study of Religion During the Cold War: East and West* (New York: Peter Lang), 119-135

Popkin, Richard H.

1990   "Polytheism, Deism, and Newton," in J. E. Force and R. H. Popkin, *Essays on the Context, Nature, and Influence of Isaac Newton's Theology* (Dordrecht: Kluwer Academic Publishers), 27-42

Powell, Mark Allan.

1998   *Jesus as a Figure in History* (Louisville: Westminster John Knox Press)

Prchlík, Ivan.

2017   "Auctor Nominis Eius Christus. Tacitus' knowledge of the origins of Christianity," *Philologica 2/ Graecolatina Pragensia*: 95-110

Price, Robert M.
2018   *Bart Ehrman Interpreted: How One Radical New Testament Scholar Understands Another* (Durham: Pitchstone Publishing)

2013-2014   [as editor] *A Wave of Hypercriticism: The English Writings of W. C. van Manen* (Valley: Tellectual Press)

2012   *The Amazing Colossal Apostle: The Search for the Historical Paul* (Salt Lake City: Signature Books)

Robertson, Archibald.
1962   *The Origins of Christianity*, Revised Edition (New York: International Publishers)

1946   *Jesus: Myth or History?* (London: Watts & Co.)

Setzer, Claudia.
1994   *Jewish Responses to Early Christians* (Minneapolis: Fortress Press)

Taylor, Robert.
1853   *The Diegesis* (Boston: J. P. Mendum)

Van Voorst, Robert.
2003   Nonexistence Hypothesis," in Leslie Houlden (ed), *Jesus in History, Thought, and Culture: An Encyclopedia* (Santa Barbara: ABC-Clio), 658-660

2000   *Jesus Outside the New Testament: An Introduction to the Ancient Evidence* (Grand Rapids: Eerdmans)

Weaver, Walter P.
1999   *The Historical Jesus in the Twentieth Century: 1900-1950* (Harrisburg: Trinity Press International)

Wells, G. A.
1969   "Stages of New Testament Criticism," *Journal of the History of Ideas* 30: 147-160

Whittaker, Thomas.
1904   *The Origins of Christianity with An Outline of Van Manen's Analysis of the Pauline Literature* (London: Watts & Co.)

Tertiary

Hansen, Christopher M.
2020   "The Evidence for Jesus, or, Why Sean McDowell is a Wolf in a Historian's Clothing," *Questions for Jesus*, https://cmcpshansen9.wixsite.com/mysite/post/the-evidence-for-jesus-or-why-sean-mcdowell-is-a-wolf-in-a-historian-s-clothing

Hurtado, Larry.
2017   "Gee, Dr. Carrier, You're Really Upset!" *Larry Hurtado's Blog* larryhurtado.wordpress.com/2017/12/07/gee-dr-carrier-youre-really-upset/

Oxford English Dictionary

2020   "pretend, v.". OED Online. June 2020. OUP.
https://www-oed-com/view/Entry/150938?rskey=Jvx3pd&result=1 (accessed, 7/27/2020)

Sunderman, Werner.
1991   "Christianity v. Christ in Manicheism,"
in *Encyclopædia Iranica*, vol. V, fasc. 5 (Costa
Mesa), 335-39.

www.ingramcontent.com/pod-product-compliance
Lightning Source LLC
Chambersburg PA
CBHW030402160726
47992CB00007B/2924